EMERGING FROM THE SMOKE

A Collection of Warrior Voices

by Orlena Fong Shek, Esq.

Edited by Dr. Linda J. Sheu

Copyright © 2022 Orlena Fong Shek, Esq..

All rights reserved. No part of this book may be used or reproduced by any means, graphic, electronic, or mechanical, including photocopying, recording, taping or by any information storage retrieval system without the written permission of the author except in the case of brief quotations embodied in critical articles and reviews.

This book is a work of non-fiction. Unless otherwise noted, the author and the publisher make no explicit guarantees as to the accuracy of the information contained in this book and in some cases, names of people and places have been altered to protect their privacy.

Archway Publishing books may be ordered through booksellers or by contacting:

Archway Publishing
1663 Liberty Drive
Bloomington, IN 47403
www.archwaypublishing.com
844-669-3957

Because of the dynamic nature of the Internet, any web addresses or links contained in this book may have changed since publication and may no longer be valid. The views expressed in this work are solely those of the author and do not necessarily reflect the views of the publisher, and the publisher hereby disclaims any responsibility for them.

Any people depicted in stock imagery provided by Getty Images are models, and such images are being used for illustrative purposes only.
Certain stock imagery © Getty Images.

Scripture quotations taken from the (NASB®) New American Standard Bible®, Copyright © 1960, 1971, 1977, 1995, 2020 by The Lockman Foundation. Used by permission. All rights reserved. www.lockman.org

ISBN: 978-1-6657-1720-5 (sc)
ISBN: 978-1-6657-1721-2 (e)

Library of Congress Control Number: 2022901792

Print information available on the last page.

Archway Publishing rev. date: 07/06/2022

Contents

Dedication vi
Warrior Poetry vii
Foreword viii
1. When I Was Four by Orlena Fong Shek 1
2. Moyamoya (Don't Wait and See) by Michelle Lochrie 3
3. Moyamoya, We Are at War by Michelle Lochrie 5
4. Moyamoya, You Did This to Me by Michelle Lochrie 6
5. Moyamoya, Together We Are Stronger by Michelle Lochrie 7
6. Well, Here We Go Again by Julie Pond 8
7. Ignorance and Shame by Shannon Yukiko Tamura 10
8. I Am by Maddy Butz 12
9. Day of Normality by Dawn Morgan 14
10. Somewhere by Jack Raymond 16
11. Seeing through the Rain by Virginia Moisant 18
12. Darkest Light by Lianne Karla A. Bigornia 20
13. The Bride of Moyamoya by Nilsa Reyna 22
14. Moyamoya Got Me Good by Neil Balbon 24
15. Stroke by John F McCullagh 26
16. Shared Aneurysm by Cailean Neal 27
17. Stroked with Love by ©Sue k Green 29
18. Help Me Find the Light by ©Sue k Green 31
19. Anywhere by ©Sue k Green 32
20. On the Strike of Stroke by ©Sue k Green 33
21. Survivor by A. Shea (Angie Waters) 34
22. I Am Reaching for Hope by A. Shea (Angie Waters) 36
23. Do Not Ask Me to Remember by Owen Darnell 37
24. Found Poetry by Jackie Byers 39
    Tree Trilogy: pages 41-43
25. Majestic Oak by Patricia Valle 41
26. Stumped by James George 42
27. Lightning Strike by Jim Christ 43
28. Go with the Flow by Tara MacInnes 45
29. Moyamoya Haikus by Mie Potter 48
30. Moyamoya Haikus by Orlena Fong Shek 50
31. When Night Descends by Orlena Fong Shek 51
32. Flowers Emerge into the Fold by Orlena Fong Shek 52
33. Out of Darkness by Orlena Fong Shek 53
34. Emergence by Orlena Fong Shek 54
35. An Unlucky Number by Orlena Fong Shek 55
Appendix 57
Resources For Stroke 59
Additional Resources 60
Resources for Caregivers 62
Glossary 64
Family Album **69**
Testimonials 77
Appreciation 81

Dedication

Dedicated with love to my husband, Justin, and to our children, Annabelle and Russell, and to the memory of my parents, Peggy and Godfrey, who taught me why we live.

Warrior Poetry

    This book emerged on October 20, 2020, when I lost my hero of a father, Godfrey Fong, as he joined his beloved wife of forty-one years, my dearly departed mother and best friend, Peggy Fong. To confront life without either of my parents living was harder than I ever imagined possible, especially when, before they left this world, I had talked to at least one of them, if not both, every day for the last forty- plus years. This book pays homage to them. May they rest in peace knowing that their daughter has emerged from the smoke.

    I am grateful to the twenty other warrior voices featured in this collection. To learn more about my co- warriors, look no further than the "warrior spotlight" following the poems. It is my hope that this book will elicit your inner warrior!

Foreword

 Most surgeons I know are equally in love with the arts as they are with science; we play music, paint, and write poetry as creative outlets to balance the rigors of our profession. We understand, as doctors, that our patients are also dynamic people who find comfort in artistic expression, particularly when complicated and difficult diseases interrupt and alter the course of their lives. When I first began treating Moyamoya thirty years ago, we didn't know much about the disease—we didn't yet realize its genetic links, its connection to other rare disorders, or the psychological impact of its symptoms on patients—but we knew that surgery and healing wouldn't be easy, and that our patients had lives they needed to get back to. I also didn't realize at the time that, over the course of treating this disease, I would develop important and long-lasting relationships with the people I treated. Relationships that went beyond the disease that introduced us to include celebrations of love and life. Now Moyamoya is connecting us in yet a new way—our shared appreciation of the arts and the creative expressions of our struggles and hopes through this beautiful collection of poetry.
 As a surgeon, my goal is to strive for the best patient outcomes by performing the correct surgical procedure with the utmost expertise in the least invasive way possible; but as a physician, my goal is to help my patients heal so they can live their best lives and pursue their dreams. It gives me great satisfaction to see my patients not only return to their lives, but to go beyond simply surviving to building new communities of support, further spreading awareness of Moyamoya, and creating art together.
 With this poetry collection, these patients are demonstrating that we have not only moved the field forward through enhanced technical precision but that we have also given patients an opportunity to create, to love, and to express their deepest feelings. I have witnessed our patients grow and become leaders in their communities, as well as motivated patient advocates who offer tremendous support to those facing the disease for the first time, and who work tirelessly to continue to expand awareness for Moyamoya internationally. We are fortunate to have had celebrities leverage their platforms to educate their audiences about Moyamoya and Moyamoya warriors dedicate their lives for legislative recognitions that enhance our work and ability to fight this disease. With the publication of this poetry collection, we are proving once again that Moyamoya doesn't mean an end to creativity and achievement, and it is in spite of this disease that people are creating beautiful new realities rooted in bravery, strength, and love.

  I remember when Orlena was transferred by ambulance to Stanford in 2011 after she suffered a devastating hemorrhage from her Moyamoya disease. We weren't sure she would survive. However, Orlena surprised us with her spirit and resolve to recuperate. We revascularized her brain in 2012, and over the last ten years, she has made a remarkable recovery. This poetry anthology, spearheaded by Orlena, is a testament to her fortitude and determination that serves to inspire us all.
  Thank you to Orlena Fong Shek for bringing the work of those affected by Moyamoya and stroke together in this wonderful collection and for allowing me to share in this project. It is my honor and privilege to have a small part in the lives of these extraordinary people who are sharing their experiences, struggles, hopes, and dreams with the world through their poems. And thank you to all Moyamoya patients and Stroke/Traumatic Brain Injury (TBI) survivors who continue to face their lives with incredible courage and who provide proof that healing is possible and that there is so much life to be lived beyond a Moyamoya or TBI diagnosis.

Gary K. Steinberg, MD, PhD
Bernard and Ronni Lacroute-William Randolph Hearst Professor of Neurosurgery and the Neurosciences
Founder and Co-Director, Stanford Stroke Center Director, Stanford Moyamoya Center
Former Chair (1995–2020), Department of Neurosurgery

Orlena Fong Shek

When I Was Four

The number 4 is considered an unlucky number in Chinese because it is nearly homophonous to the word "death" (死 pinyin: sǐ; Cantonese Yale: séi). Thus, some buildings in East Asia omit floors and room numbers containing 4, similar to the Western practice of some buildings not having a 13th floor because 13 is considered unlucky. Where East Asian and Western cultures blend, such as in Hong Kong, it is possible in some buildings that the thirteenth floor along with all the floors with 4s to be omitted. Thus a building whose top floor is numbered 100 would, in fact, have just eighty-one floors. Chinese numerology – Wikipedia

Genesis 1:19
And the evening and the morning were the fourth day.

When I was four
My sister was born, bringing my glorious reign as an only child to an abrupt end.

When I was fourteen, I spent Valentine's Day in arthroscopic surgery to remove broken cartilage in my knee after a severe patella subluxation from colliding with a classmate while playing frisbee in PE.

When I was twenty-four, I was appointed Executive Director of the UC San Diego (UCSD) Volunteer Connection, UCSD's only campus driven service organization that promotes volunteerism and organizes large scale community service projects in and around the San Diego area.

When I was thirty-four, I experienced a massive hemorrhagic stroke due to Moyamoya disease while driving my then twenty-one-month-old daughter on the freeway, followed by two bypass brain surgeries a week apart, five months later.

I can only imagine what's in store for me at age forty-four?

Orlena Fong Shek

Age: Forty-four, thirty-four at time of stroke.

Source of inspiration: The work of poets like Rainer Maria Rilke and Emily Dickinson.

Residence: California.

Stroke survivor?: Moyamoya warrior.

Occupation: Former software licensing attorney turned inspirational speaker and author, advocating positivity and resilience by utilizing a "mind over matter" mindset.

Family: Husband, twelve-year-old daughter, four-year-old son.

Hobbies: Card-making side hustle Paper Dreams, patient advocate, and aspiring poet.

Words to live by: "The potential of the mind is infinite. Use it to rise above any physical barriers you might have. Within all of us is the capacity to manifest all that we could ever need and desire by putting your mind to it."

Michelle Lochrie

Moyamoya (Don't Wait and See)

You grow in my head in silent mode,
Like a ticking time bomb
Waiting to explode.
Headaches and migraines,
strokes and TIAs,
Stealing my blood and oxygen too;
Now I know what I must do.

Surgery is my battle cry,
Angiograms and MRI;
New vessels start to grow,
Oxygen and blood begin to flow.
My battle scars I'm proud to show,
Standing tall, hand my on heart,
Brave as a warrior, I will win;
Moyamoya, I won't give in.

Our family is so strong,
In our lives you don't belong.

Michelle Lochrie

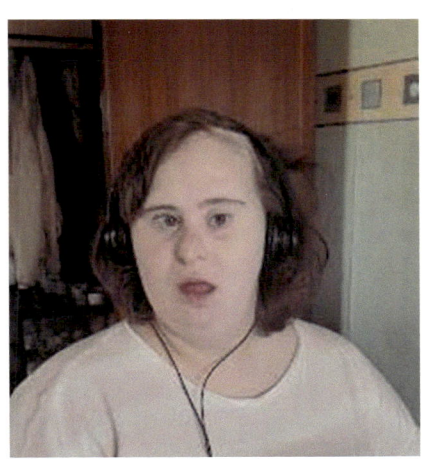

Source of inspiration: Daughter, Marie Lochrie

Age: Seventeen at time of stroke.

Residence: Scotland.

Stroke survivor?: Moyamoya warrior.

Family: Two older sisters.

Hobbies: Playing Xbox, student of living.

Words to live by: "Be happy and do not worry."

Michelle Lochrie

Moyamoya, We Are at War

Moyamoya,
We are at war.
This time you have gone too far.
Through surgery and hydration,
I am always at battle stations.

Michelle Lochrie

Moyamoya, You Did This to Me

Moyamoya,
You did this to me,
Caused me to have strokes and TIAs.

You did this to me,
Gave me left-sided paralysis.

You did this to me,
Made my speech slurred.

You did this to me,
Affected my eyesight.

You did this to me,
Gave me headaches.

You did this to me,
Made me brave—a fighter and a warrior.

You did this to me,
Moyamoya.

Michelle Lochrie

Moyamoya, Together We Are Stronger

Moyamoya family around the world,
We are few and spread afar;
Our band set in the brightest star.

Together we stand,
Like warriors in a band,
Caring, sharing love abound;
Feel the compassion going around.

Friends and family, they surround;
Our Moyamoya family is proud.
Together, we stand our ground.

Julie Pond

Well, Here We Go Again

I'm in this machine getting you scanned again.
Do you know that there are people that never even think about you?
I wish I could stop.

I sit in the dark and dream about life—it is always interrupted by you and your disease.
It is not my disease; it is yours.
I just happen to be the vessel that carries you.
At times I hate you, but without you I could not be.

Dear Brain, I am not ready yet ...
Do *not* die on me.

Julie Pond

Age: Fifty-one, diagnosed at thirty-nine.

Source of inspiration: The many MRI's and cerebral angiograms taken over the years.

Residence: Wisconsin.

Stroke survivor?: Moyamoya warrior. Total of five strokes, all of which were Moyamoya related.

Occupation: Former office manager.

Family: Two children, five step-children, and twenty grandchildren.

Hobbies: Attending Bruno Mars concerts.

Words to live by: "Drink water and mind ya business." (Bruno Mars)

Shannon Yukiko Tamura

Ignorance and Shame

For my lack of understanding,
Was I really to blame?
For the lack of awareness expanding.

For many years I rarely spoke
About a rare disease that I, too, contain;
TIAs, headaches, and stroke,
And many things that can cause emotional pain.

You've taught me to be grateful,
To be kind, understanding, and aware.
No longer will I be fearful;
I'll voice my concern and continue to share.

Misdiagnoses, complications, and fear,
Love, unity, and hope,
That's what I started to hear—
Stories of people's journey to cope.

Please tell me your stories
As I tell you my own;
The tales of our setbacks and glories,
Each day a new stepping stone.

Together let's fight on,
Continuing to trust and pray;
A new day, a new dawn,
That this, too, will end someday.

Shannon Yukiko Tamura

Age: Twenty-nine.

Source of inspiration: My journey toward the realization that I needed to spread awareness from interactions with like-minded people who understand.

Residence: Oregon.

Stroke survivor: Moyamoya warrior. TIA's for years, but no lasting stroke.

Occupation: Registered nurse in neuro critical care unit.

Family: Parents and older brother.

Hobbies: Hiking, traveling, photography.

Words to live by: "Change is a conscious effort."

Madeline Butz

I Am

I am beautiful and strong.
I wonder about zombies.
I hear my mom's voice.
I see a zoo around me.
I want a million dollars.
I am beautiful and strong.
I pretend I am flying.
I feel that there is love in the air.
I touch a cloud.
I worry about my right hand.
I cry, thinking about my cats leaving.
I am beautiful and strong.
I understand what people say.
I say that there are happily ever-after endings.
I dream about going on a date.
I try to use my right hand.
I hope to talk and use my right hand again.
I am beautiful and strong.

Madeline Butz

Age: Seventeen, age ten when experienced stroke; thirteen years old when poem was written.

Residence: Worth, IL.

Stroke survivor?: Moyamoya warrior (bilateral multiple-stroke survivor).

Hobbies: Dance, watch movies, and social media.

Words to live by: "Never give up!"

Dawn Morgan

A Day of Normality

That's all it was.
I watched you play,
Running, having fun.
Making friends, the day had just begun.
Time went by,
I could see you getting hotter;
Your face grew red,
Your hair was getting sticky.
I worried inside
Like I always do.
Just one day of fun;
It'll be ok.
Drink plenty, slow down a little,
Try and take it steady;
But that isn't you—
It just isn't possible.
Worn out and shattered,
No energy to carry on,
You spoke those dreaded words,
"I've got a headache."
An early night you had.
I hoped you would wake ok, But not today.
Washed out and pale,
"I feel confused" is what you say.
This dreaded disease is taking your childhood away.
You are wobbly on your feet;
Your hand is feeling numb.
I can see the fear;
It shows in your eyes;
I hear the pain in your cries.
I try to reassure you.
The fear is running through my own veins,
That helpless feeling all around.
Come on, my girl,
Fight it, stay strong.
Until the next one.

Dawn Morgan

Source of inspiration: Daughter, Chloe Morgan.

Residence: Wales, UK.

Stroke survivor?: Moyamoya warrior. First TIA at nine months old. Continues to have strokes, but not as severely or as frequently.

Words to live by: "I have learned to take each day as it comes and to enjoy each moment."

Jack Raymond

Somewhere

Somewhere between what she survived, and what she was becoming,
Was exactly where she was meant to be.
She was starting to love the journey
And find the comfort in the quiet corners of her wildest dreams.
They say people don't change …
Well, she wasn't always this way.
Even if she didn't change the entire world,
She would change her part of it;
And she would affect the people she shared it with.
A butterfly whose wings have been touched can indeed still fly.
Whether something was meant to be or meant to leave
Didn't matter as much anymore.
She would soak up the sun, kiss the breeze, and she would fly regardless.

Jack Raymond

Age: Thirty-five.

Source of inspiration: My actual, real life.

Residence: New Orleans.

Stroke survivor?: No.

Occupation: Author.

Hobbies: Drink, read, imagine the shittiest people in my life being kind and loving.

Words to live by or favorite motto: No words or mottos are ever worth living by.

Virginia Moisant

Seeing through the Rain

What does the sky bring into me?
Rain, drip drop, over my head.
Sometimes heavy with sorrow and fear:
What will fill my life within?
Then the rain does its job:
Brings water to wash the dust of doubt,
Bringing green new growth to reach out to stretch,
Stretch up to the sky,
Not wait to fall crashing in;
No, raise up to the sky,
Hands to hope, faith, and life to try.

Virginia Moisant

Age: Fifty.

Source of Inspiration: My faith and my family.

Residence: Oklahoma.

Stroke survivor?: Yes, unknown cause.

Occupation: Retired teacher.

Hobbies: Coloring with colored pencils.

Words to live by or favorite motto: "What we learn with pleasure we never forget." (Alfred Mercier)

Lianne Karla A. Bigornia

Darkest Light

Having aphasia is hard, but I found solace in poems and songs.

Love—pain or sweet nothings
Made my heart flutter,
Like a butterfly fresh from her cocoon.

Sadness—goodbyes or mistakes
Made my heart break as I felt every word I slowly and silently read.

But as the hours and days turned from twilight to early morn,
I fell in love with words—with every A to B to Z—
A letter slowly and surely grew stronger and clearer.
Every word had a meaning,
Had a memory,
And as I slowly gained memories and dreams,
I was even more excited of what the future would bring.

Lianne Karla A. Bigornia

Age: Thirty-five.

Source of inspiration: My loved ones—my family and my friends.

Residence: Cebu, Philippines.

Stroke survivor?: No, aphasia.

Occupation: Virtual assistant.

Hobbies: I usually watch documentaries on CuriosityStream, Netflix, or YouTube, or I read books or poems.

Words to live by or favorite motto: "Faith, hope, and love."

Nilsa Reyna

The Bride of Moyamoya

Spider webs coiling in my head.
Tiny tree branches rotting away.
Blood fighting down narrowed slides.
Poof! Puff of smoke!
*
Oh, there's a tingle.
And a burn in my arm.
But wait …
The tingle and burns just turned one.
And when did I say yes?
Do I even want to marry you?
You're mysterious and unlike anything I've ever known.
You're rare.
*
I hate this!
My fingers have gone numb.
My hand doesn't work.
My arm burns yet again.
I'm so tired.
I feel floaty.
What … is … happening?
Do I have MS?
It's something I've always feared.
*
I have an appointment next week.
It's nothing serious.
I need to go home and relax;
Self-care before the wedding.
*
Oh, our engagement is long!
You won't commit.
After six years I'm restless.
I can't wait for the honeymoon!
*
STA-MCA cranial bypass,
Dissolvable stitches, pain in my brain.
Redirected blood flow;
Twice the blood flow.
More than just a survivor bride,
I'm a Moyamoya warrior.

Nilsa Reyna

Age: Forty-five, first stroke at thirty-six.

Source of inspiration: Nature, stories of survival and hope, artists of all disciplines, and my fellow Moyamoya community.

Residence: New York.

Stroke survivor?: Moyamoya warrior.

Occupation: Actress, voice-over artist, and playwright.

Family: Partner, Bryn

Hobbies: Reading, yoga, museums, and movies.

Words to live by: "I encourage you to pay attention to what is going on in your brain. Own your power and show up for your life. Beam bright!" (Jill Bolte Taylor)

Neil Balbon

Moyamoya Got Me Good

You got me good:
You gave me stroke,
But I survive

You got me good:
I lost my speech,
But I survive

You got me good:
Doctor operated on my left brain,
But I survive

You got me good,
But I'm back to working again,
And I survive

You got me good:
I lost a lot of weight,
Still I survive

You got me good:
Now it's the right side of my brain,
But I will survive

You got me good,
But not good enough to knock me out
Because God will provide the right doctor at the right time.

Neil Balbon

Age: Forty-seven, forty-four at time of stroke.

Source of inspiration: Relationship with God.

Residence: New Orleans.

Stroke survivor?: Moyamoya warrior.

Occupation: Forklift mechanic.

Family: Wife Thea, three sons (Neil twenty-two, Noah twenty, Nathan eighteen). Thea became a neuro ICU nurse after Neil's stroke to become more familiar with neurological conditions and to support neuro patients and their loved ones.

Hobbies: Walking in the park, fishing, and cooking. Words to live by: "Thankful always."

John F. McCullagh

Stroke

The simplest word is hard to say
Once blood has leaked within the brain.
The internal fire of life has died,
Though the exterior seems the same.

He struggles saying yes or no;
He suffers visibly with pain.
His family, sadly, watches on
As the patriarch plays his endgame.

It's like a cosmic jeweler tried
To make a brilliant diamond cut;
If successful, it would have shone,
But he missed his mark and
Marred the stone.

Cailean Neal

Shared Aneurysm

Our skulls weep,
Exuding precious memories.
Our functionality seeps,
Lobotomized characters ...
The eye-spy book of life,
Now just wasted time.
Get away from me, friend?
You never cared;
We were only ever
Self-tolerating combatants.

Cailean Neel

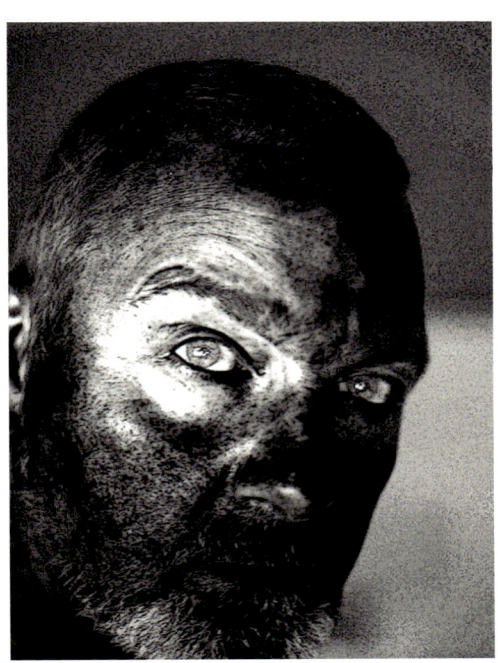

Age: 55

Source of Inspiration: Whether you are a stroke survivor or not, as a First Aider, I have attended the moment of people having had strokes a few times, and have been fascinated by the calm confusion that seems to take hold. This led me to consider what it means to lose precious memories. At present I'm working on a new website: www.blessedmemories.co.uk

Residence: UK

Hobbies: Street photography, pastel drawing and I play the Bodhran Drum

Words to live by: Life, this mystifying and precarious spark. This precious ember, so easily dampened. And yet, coddled within a sympathetic kindling, this tiny cinder may be cultivated in the most brilliant of flames.

©Sue k Green

Stroked with Love

Stroke challenged us,
Trampled on our dreams,
Rearranged our relationship,
Organized our days,
Kidnapped our future,
Extracted hope from despair.

Love finds its way through.
Overcomes the challenges,
Voices valid concerns,
Embraces our future.

©Sue k Green

I am a wife, mother, grandmother, poet, photographer …

Both poetry and photography have opened my eyes to the world around me. They have taught me to see things differently and to make new observations, and they have given me a vehicle of expression that I never knew before.

As a senior and caregiver to my husband, who is recovering from a stroke he suffered over nine years ago, "precious moments" seem all important to capture. I have never been one to overtly show my emotions, but as I travel my newest emotional roller coaster, I have learned that emotions are just a part of each of us—they need not be justified—and it helps when I share.

At first, poetry was just therapeutic for me. Now, I am reading and studying poetry as an art form. I have so much to learn, and I find it truly a challenge. There is so much to be said about the world in which we live. Poetry affords us the vehicle with which to share an emotion, an opinion, or open a new line of reasoning. I believe it offers me some sense of control in an otherwise chaotic world.

©Sue k Green

Help Me Find the Light

I am hungry, Yearning for way past The dark tunnel, Searching for light;
Stroke has captured my senses, Challenged my simplest move, Willed me to find meaning
In this new challenge. My independence adrift,
Thankful for the compassion of others, Adhere to serve, care,
And help me find the light.

©Sue k Green

Anywhere

Anywhere, Anyplace, Anytime with you.
Before your stroke, You survived,
And although I'm here With you to face
Your every challenge, We walk in
Two different worlds; If only that could change.

©Sue k Green

On the Strike of Stroke

On the lightning strike of stroke,
The life and death of common folk,
Weathering changes so severe,
Challenging winds that others fear.

Walking paths midst hidden signposts
Complete with snare of hefting hosts,
Learning anew the walk and language,
Awakening travel 'round lumbering baggage.

Dreams and plans out with the storm,
Rains of doubt now more the norm;
Effort, challenge, new encounter,
Each day waking with fear of flounder.

Angie A. Shea (Angie Waters)

Survivor

Yes ... I am a survivor;
With every breath, I will be,
But it is as a fighter
I pray you will remember me.
Not for my life's struggles,
But for the way I gave them beauty.

Angie A. Shea (Angie Waters)

Age: Forty-nine.

Source of inspiration: Poetry has been a part of my life since early childhood when I first started writing. In my teens, the few books I had from classic romantic poets really stole my heart. Now, the inspiration is endless from my own life struggles with chronic illness and past trauma. My health is compromised by Lupus SLE (Systemic Lupus Erythematosus) to the point that I am no longer able to keep a regular job. It includes seizures, heart issues, chronic migraines, extreme brain fog, immobility, and many other complications. I am currently on disability and doing my best to create a life I can be proud of, in spite of Lupus, by writing and creating art.

Residence: Georgia.

Family: I have two grown boys that are my heart and were my motivation for many years. Now, I am chasing my own dreams and enjoying the opportunities that have arisen thus far as well as finding hope for the future.

Hobbies: When I'm not working at that, I enjoy the outdoors, art museums, travel, and reading. You can find my work on Facebook at www.facebook.com/a.sheawriter and Instagram @a.shea_writerName.

Words to live by: "Those who have a 'why' to live, can bear with almost any 'how.'" (Friedrich Nietzsche)

Angie A. Shea (Angie Waters)

I Am Reaching for Hope

Amidst the chaos
Of dreams and reality,
The past is falling away;
And (for once)
I am not focused on the debris.
I am looking up ...
My eyes have a death grip
On the sky.
I am not letting go
(come what may).
Every day,
I
Will
Rise.

Owen Darnell

Do Not Ask Me to Remember

Do not ask me to remember;
Don't try to make me understand;
Let me rest and know you're with me;
Kiss my cheek and hold my hand.

I'm confused beyond your concept;
I am sad and sick and lost.
All I know is that I need you
To be with me at all cost.

Do not lose your patience with me;
Do not scold or curse or cry.
I can't help the way I'm acting,
Can't be different though I try.

Just remember that I need you,
That the rest of me is gone;
Please don't fail to stand beside me,
Love me till my life is done.

Owen Darnell

In 1994, when his wife of forty years, Esther Darnell, died, Capt. Darnell found a way to help others coping with similar problems and loss by becoming a prominent advocate for Alzheimer's caregivers. He wrote "Do Not Ask Me to Remember" in honor of his wife, and it is often referred to as the "Alzheimer's Poem."

Jackie Byers

Found Poetry

Originally, with a fast brain and deft fingers,
With nothing to lose in the chaos of fire,
With death so close, inside my head,
God's special grace saved my life.
The greatest prize of all: extra living,
Destiny that day.

Jackie Byers

Age: Fifty-seven, fifty and fifty-one at time of strokes.

Source of inspiration: My inspiration is just my imagination, which still runs rampant even after Moyamoya! (Thank God!)

Residence: Texas.

Occupation if any: Mixed media artist.

Family members: Husband, Rick, and Daughter, Madison, age thirty-two, who is a special education teacher.

Stroke survivor?: Moyamoya warrior (six major strokes before Moyamoya diagnosis).

Hobbies: I enjoy creating art, listening to music, traveling, gardening, etc.

Words to live by: "Life is good!"

Patricia Valle

Majestic Oak

Standing proud in the quiet woodlands,
The majestic oak stretches upward toward the sky,
Spreading its mighty branches as leaves
Give shelter from the heat of the sun.
As the season changes to autumn,
Leaves turn a golden hue of yellow-brown,
While a variety of wildlife gather fallen acorns,
Providing food that lies on dry ground.

When winter winds batter the old oak tree,
Blowing its leaves in all directions,
Massive branches stand stark and naked
As new falling snow glistens in moonlit sky.
As the scene changes, new growth bursts forth;
Spring arrives to the sound of nature's melody.
A clear rippling brook, flowing so free,
Just a short distance from the majestic oak tree.

Copyright 2003, Patricia Valle

James George

Stumped

A tall tree stood on a hill,
And it was my favorite.
Like my brother,
Lightning struck it,
And it quivered and shook.
Like my brother,
Its limbs still wave,
And the trunk stands.
Like my brother,
It has lost most leaves
And is stiff and still.
Like my brother,
The brain inside is alive
But without words on lips.
He's my brother.

Jim Christ

Lightning Strike

It stands twisted
As if dodging bullets
In slo-mo, and in fact
Had on several occasions.
Age-old earth-moored trunk
Reaching and cascading upward
In suspended freeze frame,
Stuttering
When winds make it tremble.
It is bark-covered branches of lightening,
Emerging wooden, bright, and filling sky,
Reaching out with jagged strokes
From earthen cloud below.

Jim Christ

Age: 70

Residence: Santa Rosa

Occupation: Flooring Inspector

Stroke survivor? Never had a stroke myself

Family: Single at this time

Hobbies: Watching sports, contemplating humanity

Words to live by: "Where I think; I am" (borrowed from Descartes and modified to fit my "vie")

Tara MacInnes

Go with the Flow

.
.
.
.
.

"Go with the flow," or so they say. But what if the flow isn't going?
What if the norm became abnormal and commonplace became rare?

.

Rare is but an evolutionary word, ever changing, never-settling, always subjective.
With awareness, what once was "rare" no longer is. But change, first, is necessary.

.

What if the world shook and the ground beneath you cracked? What if the
world as you knew it no longer existed and a "new normal" began?

.

From cracks in concrete have sprouted the most beautiful flowers, their root systems
hidden, yet well- established. What if cracks in healthcare left something to be
desired? Such is true for Moyamoya patients. But, what if it didn't have to be?

.

What if hands of time stood still and never ran out, like sand in an hourglass? What if
medically gifted, specialized hands were plentiful and not as rare as the illness itself?

.

Life is a gift, and I pray blessings find you in the collateral beauty, pain, and
damage of it all. I pray faith is not lost on you in fear and frustration.

.

What if blood flow was restored before it ran out? What if time, for
once, worked in your favor, and lives were never cut short?

.

Early diagnoses precede better prognoses. In the highlands and the heartaches
of every mountain, valley, and sea, as long as there is air in my lungs, blood
freely flowing to my brain, and words in my mouth, I will advocate.

.

What if medical culture transitioned from reactive to attentive and preventative care? What if patients' words were never doubted, the need for care never questioned, and compassion was plentiful? There was rest for the weary, recovery from trials, reprieve of symptoms, relief from hardships, respite care for caregivers who saw their loved ones through obstacles time and time again, and redemption for humanity.

.

What if "Moyamoya" was more than a softly spoken, mispronounced utterance in medical school when read from a textbook paragraph?

.

All lives matter. Blood flow matters. Time matters. Brain matter matters. You matter. *Yes*, you matter.

.

What if we didn't judge patients or books by their outward appearances? What if we were no longer mislead by what meets the eye and strove to understand the root cause?

.

It's what's on the inside that counts. When you get down to it, we all have brains and bleed the same.

.

What if indifference and lack of understanding turned into floods of awareness and ripple effects? What if overwhelming support, empathy, and resources were capable of pushing out negative aspects of being identified as "rare"? What if stereotyping stroke patients didn't exist? Empowered people empower others. In the same way fellow patients have empowered me, I hope this empowers you.

.

What if we really could "go with the flow" because everyone, the world round, had the blood flow their brain needed?

.

Hope can seem fleeting, like wind passing through trees outside a hospital-room window. But in the darkest of times and farthest reaches of the world, hope is the most important thing to hold onto. It's powerful, and when the weight of the world is too much, hope carries you through. I plead you never lose sight of hope.

.

What if we could do away with the "What if's?" because Moyamoya awareness existed everywhere and sufficient holistic care was not the exception?

.

Everywhere, Moyamoya awareness. Now, go with the flow.

Tara MacInnes

Age: Thirty-four.

Source of inspiration: Collaborating with like-minded, passionate individuals who selflessly serve the Moyamoya, stroke, rare disease, and special needs communities.

Residence: Georgia.

Stroke survivor?: Moyamoya warrior. Bilateral ischemic strokes in early childhood. Properly diagnosed with Moyamoya upon Moyamoya induced stroke at age seventeen.

Occupation: Adaptive, special needs swim instructor, specializing in working with children whose needs range from physical to mental health.

Hobbies: Tara and her husband, Sean, enjoy spending time with veterans and their families, attending church, spending time with their dog (also a stroke "fur-vivor"), gardening, bonfires with friends and family, and going to the beach. Sean is a fellow stroke survivor, brain-surgery patient, and advocate. His hemorrhagic stroke was caused by an undetected brain aneurysm rupturing in his early-twenties when he was on active Coast Guard duty. They met as a result of their mutual stroke experiences and advocacy efforts. You can follow their story via #FlirtingWithStrokes.

Words to live by: "Although the world is full of suffering, it is also full of overcoming it." (Helen Keller)

Mie Potter

Moyamoya Strong

Moyamoya strong,
Badge of a survivor stands
Living in the now.

Wind Bends a Birch

Wind bends a birch,
We adjust with each challenge,
Learning so we thrive.

Mie Potter

Age: Fifty-seven, brain bleed at forty-one.

Residence: South Carolina.

Stroke survivor?: Moyamoya warrior.

Occupation: Personal and business coach.

Family members: Her children, Allen (twenty-six) and John (twenty-four).

Hobbies: Walk, read, explore.

Words to live by: "You may not control all the events that happen to you, but you can decide not to be reduced by them." (Maya Angelou, "Letter to My Daughter")

Orlena Fong Shek

Moyamoya Haikus

It's a Puff of Smoke!
Then a hemorrhagic stroke
Moyamoya strong

Hemiparesis
On left side of the body
Rehabilitate

Headaches and Numbness
Previously a mystery
Sudden clarity

Moyamoya Girl
Confronted with brain disease
Defying all odds

Life Interrupted
With stroke and a surgery
Emerging with strength

Such a Miracle
Living with Moyamoya
We are survivors

A Rare Brain Disease
Called Moyamoya disease
Discover a cure

Lacking Good Blood Flow
The brain needed a bypass
Now a Warrior

Imagine a World
Where there is no death from Stroke
Moyamoya free

Orlena Fong Shek

When Night Descends

When night descends
On the city
Where you live now,
Don't be afraid if it shrouds the truth
That was meant to set you free.
Dance into the darkness with your partner
To keep time with hope
Because, when morning breaks
Amid the stillness of your faith,
We will carry on.

Orlena Fong Shek

Flowers Emerge into the Fold

Dandelions whisper
Through the void
To uncover the darkness
And let free the moon.
In those quiet waves of strength,
You know how much you are worth

Orlena Fong Shek

Out of Darkness

Wash away the heaviness that lines the contours of your soul
Until it's as light as an alabaster sunset.
Forest fires may burn
Amid a pandemic,
During times like this
You fight to rewrite each story into a triumph.

Orlena Fong Shek

Emergence

After surgery,
Groggy, but sudden clarity.
A brain transformed
Through careful bypass and rearrangement of blood flow.
Restoration
For the first time
In thirty-four years—
A reckoning.
Find the light
In a world of darkness,
Piercing through the deep abyss
To ignite a fire
Of unknown desire.
Decreased life expectancy,
Increased expectancy to live—
Warrior
Emerging from the smoke.

Orlena Fong Shek

An Unlucky Number

Why is number four
Such an unlucky number?
Reclaiming it mine,
What might seem unlucky
May actually bring you luck
In ways never imagined possible.

The number 8

4+4= 8 (八, BĀ) - LUCKY

8 is the luckiest number in Chinese culture because 八 sounds like 發 (fa), which means "wealth", "fortune", and "prosper" in Chinese. Multiples of eight are even better, as 88 bears a resemblance to 囍(shuāng xǐ), or "double happiness". While the Chinese will go to great lengths to avoid 4 in daily life, they will try to incorporate 8 wherever they can. In the Beijing summer Olympics, the opening ceremony began at 8:08 pm on 8/8/08. Since the number 8 is believed to bring good luck, many airlines in Chinese-speaking countries will use combinations of 8 as flight numbers. – Tutor Ming China Expats & Culture Blog

Appendix

COVER ART EXPLAINED
Designed by Mariah Dingman

Moyamoya means a "puff of smoke" in Japanese, its country of origin. The appearance of a "puff of smoke" is a description of the appearance of a Moyamoya brain on MRA (Magnetic Resonance Angiography), in which the diseased vessels are small, weak, and prone to bleeding, resulting in potentially devastating hemorrhagic stroke

The cover art incorporates an actual MRA scan of a Moyamoya brain combined with an artistic rendering of various stroke survivors/warriors "emerging" from the "puff of smoke," with one such warrior representation being the author herself.

The blue background is in the official "Moyamoya Blue" color. The gold is a nod to the meaning behind the author's name "Orlena," a name of French origin meaning gold. Orlena's parents believed in the Chinese Five Elements Theory, which holds that the five elements—metal, fire, wood, earth, and water—are the fundamental elements in the universe between which all interactions occur. At the time of Orlena's birth, her Father consulted this theory and the only element lacking was metal. Orlena's parents sought to "replenish" metal by naming her "Orlena."

~ MOYAMOYA DISEASE ~

An Occlusive Cerebrovascular Disorder

Moyamoya is one of the rarest forms of occlusive cerebrovascular disorders encountered in neurosurgery. In patients with Moyamoya, blood vessels proliferate around a blocked artery in an attempt to bypass an occlusion. The appearance of these vessels on a cerebral angiogram resembles a "puff of smoke" or "Moyamoya", a term coined by a Japanese team who first described the disease. Moyamoya can affect children and adults -- with symptoms of TIAs, strokes, headaches and seizures. There is no effective drug treatment. Surgery is aimed at bypassing the blockage with another artery to restore blood flow.

Resources For Stroke

What to do when a person has a stroke:

Even if you have already had a stroke, it's important for you and your loved ones to know the signs and symptoms for stroke. If you experience any of these signs and symptoms, call 911 immediately. Keep in mind that these signs and symptoms may go away and then come back.

1. **Perform CPR if necessary**
2. **Note the time you first see symptoms**
3. **Sudden numbness or weakness in the face, arm, or leg (often on one side of the body)**
4. **Sudden confusion or trouble understanding what is going on**
5. **Sudden blurred or decreased vision in one or both eyes**
6. **Sudden difficulty speaking, understanding speech, or reading**
7. **Sudden trouble with walking, loss of balance, dizziness, or problems with coordination**
8. **Sudden, severe headache for no reason**
9. **Fainting or seizures**

From *Climbing The Mountain: Stories of Hope and Healing after Stroke and Brain Injury*, edited by Candis Fancher, Lindsey McDivitt, and Jacquelyn B. Fletcher

Additional Resources

Stanford Moyamoya Center
https://stanfordhealthcare.org/medical-clinics/neuroscience
213 Quarry Road
Palo Alto, CA 94304 Phone: (650)723-5575
The Stanford Moyamoya Center offers a highly experienced group of professionals who see several new Moyamoya patients each week, making Stanford the largest Moyamoya referral center in the world.

May 6th World Moyamoya Day Facebook Group
https://www.facebook.com/groups/145861575578487
This page is for everyone worldwide to come together to recognize World Moyamoya Day. This will be (unofficially, for now) May 6th each year: Our own special day to do what we need to do—celebrate the life and health we have, honor those who have fallen, and recognize the common thread that has brought us together. My hope is that, as a group, even with hundreds to thousands of miles between us, we can increase awareness, ultimately leading to better outcomes for people stricken with this rare disease.

Pacific Stroke Association
www.pacificstrokeassociation.org
Since its inception, PSA's mission has been to reduce the incidence of stroke through education and to help alleviate stroke's devastating aftermath through support programs for stroke survivors and family caregivers. Pacific Stroke Association is a local, community-based, nonprofit organization serving Santa Clara and San Mateo counties.
Phone: (650)565-8485
Champion the Challenges
https://www.championthechallenges.org/about/
Our mission is to reimagine stroke rehabilitation for the world.
Stroke Awareness Oregon
www.strokeawarenessoregon.org
A nonprofit created by physicians, stroke patients, and community members—exists to make a real difference. Stroke treatment and care is seeing advances but challenges still exist. A person hit by a stroke often transpires too late to fully benefit from new medical advances. People surviving a stroke and completing rehabilitation are returned to the community without clear direction, follow-up, or support.
Phone: (541)323-5641

Local Acute Rehab Hospitals:
Stanford Stroke Center: 780 Welch Road, Suite 205, Palo Alto, CA 94301
Phone: (650)723-4448
Kentfield Hospital: 1125 Sir Francis Drake Blvd., Kentfield, CA 94904
Phone: (415)456-9680
Santa Clara Valley Medical Center: 761 Bascom Ave., Willow Glen, CA 95128
Phone: (888)334-1000

Local Outpatient Therapy Services:
Mills-Peninsula Health Services, San Mateo, CA
Phone: (650)696-4317
Santa Clara Valley Medical Center, San Jose, CA
Phone: (888)334-1000
Neuro-IFRAH Center and Clinics, Foster City, CA
Phone: (650)286-9030
Stanford Neurologic Rehabilitation Program, Palo Alto, CA
Phone: (650)725-5106
UCSF Medical Center at Mission Bay outpatient therapy
Services: https://www.ucsfmissionbayhospitals.org/outpatient
Support for Stroke Survivors:
American Stroke Association, a division of the American Heart Association
1-888-4STROKE (478-7653)
www.StrokeAssociation.org

Resources for Caregivers

Family Caregiver Alliance
Phone: 1-800-445-8106
www.caregiver.org
National Family Caregivers Association
Phone: 1-800-896-3650
www.nfacares.org **Today's Caregiver**
Phone: 1-800-829-2734
www.caregiver.com

Medical and Adaptive Equipment:
ABLEDATA
Phone: 1-800-227-0216
www.abledata.com

Adaptability Catalogue (S&S Worldwide)
Phone: 1-800-266-8856
AliMed catalogue
Phone: 1-800-225-2610
www.slimed.com
Enrichments catalogue (Sammons Preston)
Phone: 1-800-323-5547
North Coast Medical Catalogue
Phone: 1-800-821-93193

Sign up for *Stroke Connection* magazine—helpful tips for daily self-care and many free informational brochures.

Brain Injury Association of America Phone: 1-800-444-6443
www.biausa.org

Christopher and Dana Reeve Paralysis Resource Center
www.paralysiscenter

Meals on Wheels Association of America
Phone: (703)548-5558
www.mowaa.org

My Medicine List
www.mnpatientsafety.org
Provides a form to help track medications

National Aphasia Association
Phone: 1-800-922-4622
www.aphasia.org
National Institute of Neurological Disorders and Stroke
www.ninds.nih.gov/disorders/stroke/stroke.htm

National Stroke Association
Phone: 1-800-STROKES (787-6537)
www.stroke.org
Sign up for *Stroke Smart* magazine.

QUITPLAN
Phone: 1-888-354-PLAN (7526)
www.quitplan.quitnet.com
Tobacco Quit Line, providing free counseling over the phone.

From Climbing The Mountain: Stories of Hope and Healing After Stroke and Brain Injury
Edited by Candis Fancher, Lindsey McDivitt, and Jacquelyn B. Fletch

Glossary

Acute Stroke: A stage of stroke that starts at the beginning of symptoms and lasts for a few hours after. **Agnosia:** The inability to process and recognize sensory information, like recognizing objects, persons, shapes, or smells. It is not memory loss.

Aneurysm: A weak or thin spot of an artery wall that has ballooned out from the wall and filled with blood.

Anomia: Difficulty in naming objects or retrieving a desired word.

Aphasia: Difficulty in understanding and stating language, resulting from injury to the speech and language areas of the brain. It affects reading, writing, speaking, and listening.

Arteriovenous Malformation (AVM): Unusual tangles of blood vessels that cause multiple irregular connections between the arteries and veins.

Carotid Artery: An artery, located on either side of the neck, which supplies the front part of the brain with blood.

Central Stroke Pain (Central Pain Syndrome): Pain that can occur after stroke as a result of damage to an area in the brain called the thalamus. The pain can be a mixture of sensations, including heat and cold.

Dissection: A tear in the inside wall of a blood vessel that can block blood flow or cause blood clots that may cause a stroke.

Deep Vein Thrombosis (DVT): A blood clot that forms in a vein deep in the body. It can cause a potentially life-threatening complication if the clot detaches and moves to the lungs, resulting in a blockage known as a pulmonary embolism (PE) (see definition below).

Dysarthria: Difficulty saying words clearly due to problems with muscle strength and coordination. **Dysphagia:** Difficulty with swallowing.

Edema: Swelling.

Embolic Stroke: A stroke caused by an embolus (a free-floating mass traveling through the bloodstream). The embolus may be a blood clot (thrombus), a ball of fat, a bubble of air or other gas (gas embolism), or foreign material.

Embolus: A clot, plaque, or other material that travels from one vessel in the body to another. A stroke caused by a clot that forms in the heart and then goes to the brain is called an embolic stroke or cardioembolic stroke.

Endothelial Wall: A flat layer of cells that make up the inside lining of a blood vessel.
Hemiparesis: Weakness on one side of the body.

Hemiplegia: Complete paralysis on one side of the body.

Hemorrhagic Stroke: Sudden bleeding into or around the brain. It is also called a brain hemorrhage or brain bleed.

High-Density Lipoprotein (HDL): Also known as "good cholesterol." HDL helps move the "bad cholesterol" from the arteries back to the liver so it can break down and leave the body.

Hyperlipidemia (High Cholesterol): Too many lipids (fat) in the blood. Cholesterol and triglycerides (another fat) can form plaque between artery walls, causing a blockage or a clot that can travel throughout the body and increase the risk of a heart attack or stroke.

Hypertension (High Blood Pressure): Persistently high arterial (artery) blood pressure. This means a measurement greater than or equal to 140 mm/Hg systolic (top number) pressure over 90 mm/Hg diastolic (bottom number) pressure.

Homonymous Hemianopia (visual field cut): A loss of vision in the same visual field in both eyes. This type of partial blindness is caused by injury to the brain.

Hypoxia: A state of decreased oxygen delivery to a cell so that the oxygen falls below normal levels. **Infarct:** An area of tissue that is dead because of a loss of blood supply

Intracerebral Hemorrhage (ICH): A type of stroke that occurs when a vessel within the brain leaks blood into the brain.

Ischemic Penumbra: Areas of damaged but still living brain cells arranged in a patchwork pattern around areas of dead brain cells.

Ischemic Stroke: Damage to the brain caused by lack of blood flow usually from a clot.

Lacunar Infarction: Blockage of a small artery deep in the brain resulting in a small area of damaged brain tissue.

Large Vessel Disease: Abnormalities in the large brain arteries.

Low-Density Lipoprotein (LDL): Also known as the "bad cholesterol." A compound that carries most of the total cholesterol in the blood and deposits the excess along the inside of arterial walls.

Micro Hemorrhage: A tiny area of bleeding in brain tissue.

Muscle Tone: Contraction of a muscle or the muscle's resistance to a stretch during a resting state. **Muscle Tension:** Muscles of the body remain semi-contracted for a period of time in the resting state. **Neuroplasticity:** The potential for the brain to reorganize and adapt as needed by creating new neural pathways.

Verbal Apraxia: A speech difficulty that results in errors in speech production. There is no paralysis responsible for the problem. Apraxic speech, unlike dysarthric speech, is characterized by distortions in sounds and by substitutions or additions of sounds and syllables.

May I write words more naked than flesh,
Stronger than bone, more resilient than sinew, sensitive than nerve.

—**Sappho**

Dr. Linda J. Sheu, Editor

Dr. Sheu is a dermatologist in the San Francisco Bay Area. Her love of the humanities and the philosophy of medicine rendered her an inspirational and integral part of the editorial process of *Emerging from the Smoke: A Collection of Warrior Voices*. Revered in the community for their family values of unconditional love, wisdom and integrity, Linda's mother and father are a constant source of inspiration as she raises her two young children. Based in the San Francisco Bay Area, Linda lives with her loving family and her two young children.